Alhambra *of Granada*

THE ART OF ARCHITECTURE

PHOTOGRAPHS: CARLOS GIORDANO RODRÍGUEZ AND NICOLÁS PALMISANO SOSA

DOSDE PUBLISHING

Contents

The origins

During the thirteenth century the Muslim presence in the Iberian peninsula suffered a sharp decline due to rivalries between the different families who aspired to control the territory and owing to the efficacy of the expansionist policy undertaken by the Christian monarchs. The last stronghold of Islamic power was the Nasrid kingdom, founded in 1232 by Muhammad I –also known as Ibn Al-Ahmar, "the son of the red"–, who managed to retain its independence by means of one-off smart policy alliances with the Castilian Crown and North African leaders. In 1238 the Sultan established the headquarters of his court in Granada –which during the eleventh century had been the capital of another Muslim dynasty, the Zirids–, on some old fortifications that were on the Sabika hilltop, one of Sierra Nevada's foothills. This was the origin of the Alhambra –"the red one" in Arabic–, a large fortified enclosure which, thanks to the refurbishments carried out by successive Nasrid sultans, steadily expanded until it formed a complex urban network and turned into one of the most influential royal cities of the period, equipped with luxurious palaces, administrative buildings, mosques, schools, prisons, gardens, baths and workshops. From the fifteenth century, the Moorish kingdom of Granada stepped into a phase of internal instability and was progressively losing territories, caused by the relentless pressure from its rivals. Finally, after a hard siege, in the year 1492 Sultan Boabdil handed the keys of the city over to the Catholic Monarchs, who retained the Alhambra as a symbol of their victory, thereby perpetuating the importance of a monumental arrangement unique in the world.

Architectonic icon
Situated on the Sabika hilltop, the Alhambra converted into the landmark of the city of Granada.

A sum of constructions

Muslim leaders often used architecture as a way of displaying their rank and by setting themselves apart from their rivals. This competitiveness was reflected in the challenging structural creations of the successive tenants of the Alhambra, who did not hesitate to carry out comprehensive renovations in the residences erected by their predecessors, enlarging and modifying them with new ornamental elements, or even abandoning them to replace them with more sumptuous palaces. In such a way, Granada's great architectural ensemble transformed into a vast arrangement of juxtaposed constructions that did not follow a preconceived architectonic scheme and which took on different uses according to the changing requirements of its residents.

1. The Alhambra and Granada
Fragment of an engraving by Hoefnagel from 1575.

2. The Court of the Lions
Engraving by David Roberts dating around 1835.

Entrances and towers

Since ancient times, urban centres associated with political power were provided with walls, fortified gates and towers that, apart from fulfilling a defensive purpose, acquired a symbolic value, projecting an intimidating image whilst acting as a barrier –whether physically or imaginary– between the outside world and the space inhabited by those who governed. Planned in a historical context that was marked by political instability and constant border conflicts, the Alhambra had to demonstrate its robustness and resistance, in such a way that its developers devised a thick wall with a 2,200 metre long perimeter that incorporated all the techniques developed by Muslims in the field of military architecture, such as the barbican –a low wall which, in case of an enemy incursion, would act as the first line of defence– or the sentry walk –a narrow walkway circumnavigating the upper section of the fortress with crenellations to crouch and shelter behind–, amongst other solutions. With the aim of reinforcing the wall, diverse towers were erected, distributed in an irregular way and separated with just enough distance so that word could be spread in case of an attack. Moreover, four of these towers were provided with gateways to the complex, two located on the northern side –the Arms Tower and the Arrabal one– and two others on the southern side –the Seven Floor Tower and the Justice one–, with a design that meant that a large number of attackers could be effectively fended off without the need for many defenders. Thanks to a combination of all these elements, the Alhambra became an impregnable fortress and the security of the inhabitants of Granada was guaranteed.

Symbolism
The entrance ways combine their defence function with allegorical details, such as the shells on the Gate of Justice, symbolic of life.

The Gate of Justice

1348 Sultan Yusuf I
dered the construc-
on of the Alhambra's
ost imposing gate,
uated on the south-
n wall of the palatine
ty. The importance
this entranceway –
amed *Bab al-Sharía* in
rabic, an expression
hich translates to the
ate of Justice or Espla-
ade– was reflected by
e symbolic ornamen-
tion of the façade.
n the entrance's exte-
or arch there is a lintel
hich is decorated with
carving of a hand,
terpreted both as
sign of protection and
rength as well as a
ference to the five
ndamental precepts
Islam –faith, prayer,
ms, fasting and pil-
image–, whilst the
ey depicted on the lin-
l of the interior arch
ssibly means that a
cred space is about to
e entered.

>>
The Gate of the Seven Floors

Known in the Islamic era as *Bab al-Gudur* –the Gate of the Wells– the Gate of the Seven Floors was constructed in the fourteenth century over a smaller one in order to provide a monumental entrance way to the upper area o the *Medina* of the Alhambra. Formed by a cubic tower erected over three circular vaults, it most likely carried out a ceremonial function for the Nasrids, given that chronicles indicate that it acted as the stage for great military parades. In the year 1812 it was practically destroyed by Napoleonic troops during their withdrawl from Granada, in such a way that it then had to be reconstructed in the latter half of the twentieth century with the aid of ancient etchings.

<<
The Gate of Justice

Elements such as the plant engravings on the capitals of the interior archway show off the skill of Nasrid craftsmanship.

Tower of the Points
Used in order to defend the Gate of the Arrabal, its corbels helped support the machicolations, whose openings were used to attack the enemy from.

The towers

Diverse watchtowers were erected along the site's walls in order to centralise incidences detected by sentries who surveilled the inside and outside of the Alhambra. Located at strategic points, these constructions broke up the outline of the sentry walk, in such a way that those who walked around the high part of the wall were obliged to go past a control post. Deprived of any ornamental detail, this type of fortification –which the Tower of the Judge (*Torre del Qadí*) belongs to, which controlled access into the Generalife area– co-existed with another model of construction set aside for residential use, such as the Tower of the Captive and the Tower of the Princesses, whose interiors were provided with all the comforts and luxuries expected of a residence that was to be used by someone holding a high position in the Court.

Tower of the Captive
During the first half of the fifteenth century, coinciding with one of the periods of intense construction of the Alhambra, Sultan Yusuf I ordered the Tower of the Captive to be built, which is said to be named after Isabel de Solís, the favourite and wife of King Muley Hacén, who is thought to have been imprisoned there. With little to differentiate its exterior from the rest of the towers, its interior follows a decoration scheme particular to that of Nasrid palaces, with a courtyard adorned with peralted arches that lead the way to a richly decorated salon of square ground plan that has bedchambers on three of its sides.

Tower of the Princesses

Erected under the reign of Muhammad VII, between the years 1392 and 1408, and the setting for the tales of writer Washington Irving, the Tower of the Princesses is considered to be one of the last major constructions of the Alhambra's Nasrid period. Just like the Tower of the Captive, its smooth, plain walls hide an interior of sumptuous and opulent design, in line with its eminently residential purpose. Accessible from a curved corridor covered by a vault with *mocárabe* work, the area is assembled around a square-shaped courtyard presided over by a polygonal marble fountain that connects with three bedrooms.

Alcazaba

During their rapid expansion over the Iberian peninsula, the Muslims often settled in cities where they were outnumbered in respect to the local Christian population. In order to consolidate their rule and avoid armed conflicts, the conquerors instigated the construction of fortified areas known as *alcazabas* (translated as fortress or citadel), which were segregated from the rest of the urban nucleus and which provided accommodation for the ruling classes as well as an important part of the army. In the eleventh century, when Granada was under the control of the Zirid dynasty, the *alcazaba* was located on the hilltop of Albaicín, a space which had been in use since the Iberian period. Two centuries later, with the establishment of the Nasrid kingdom and the arrival of Sultan Muhammad I, this site grew unsafe owing to the dense urban area, resulting in the centre of power being shifted to the opposite hill, the Sabika, which had most likely housed military constructions before the Muslims settled. Parting from a triangular ground-plan, the fortress erected by the Nasrids took advantage of part of the old fortifications that still remained on the western area of the Sabika, adding elements of great strategic importance to the fortress's walls such as the Broken Tower (*Torre Quebrada*), the Homage Tower (*Homenaje*) and the Watch Tower (*Vela*). Likewise, army installations and houses were built inside the citadel that protected the Sultan and the rest of the inhabitants of the Alhambra, which was able to expand and fulfil its potential thanks to being shielded by this architectural complex which was as functional as it was imposing.

Formal sobriety
With a square ground plan, the towers built in the Nasrid period stand out for their plainness, in accordance with the Alcazaba's military use.

Military district
The centre of the Alcazaba was originally taken up by an urban stretch designed for the use of the army that was responsible for defending the Alhambra. According to what was discovered from the foundations unveiled in the 20th century, it can be deduced that the neighbourhood was probably based around a longitudinal street that divided the site into two quite different areas: on the north side were properties of different sizes organised around courtyards –a typical feature of Hispano-Muslim architecture–, whilst on the south side were annexes for the troops. Warehouses, dungeons, an oven and a steam bath completed the structure of the arrangement.

Gate of Arms

The main entrance of the Alcazaba was found on the northern wall, where in the thirteenth century the Gate of Arms (*Puerta de Armas*) was constructed –*Bib Silah* in Arabic–, which citizens passed through that came from the urban centre situated on the Albaicín Hill. Its owes its name to the fact that before entering the site, visitors – closely watched by guards– had to put down their arms as a sign of peace. With a curved design in order to facilitate its defence, the gate had two exits: one connected with the palace zone and the Medina, whilst the other connected with the Alcazaba, which was reached by following a narrow route.

An impregnable site
The layout of the towers and the presence of elements such as crenellations and moats meant the fortress could be defended in an efficient way from all sides.

Christian adaptations

After the Catholic Monarchs conquered Granada in 1492, the Alcazaba was subject to diverse refurbishments which were carried out in order to adapt its defensive system to new military techniques. The growing use of artillery led to the construction of bulwarks and bastions such as the Cube Tower (*Torre del Cubo*), built over a former Muslim tower based on a circular ground plan, more appropriate

for protection against enemy fire. These remodelings of military character were also accompanied by an intervention of civil character on the eastern side of the site, where a gully was filled in so that a large cistern could be installed for guaranteeing the citadel's water supply. With a capacity of more than 1,600 cubic metres, this water tank ended up converting into the base of the esplanade known as the Plaza de los Aljibes.

The Watchtower

With a height reaching around twenty-seven metres, the Alcazaba's highest tower was planned in the thirteenth century on the far western end of the site. At the bottom of the watchtower was a basement that was used as a silo or dungeon, which was then topped with three floors that were provided with side galleries which gradually increased in size as the tower rose in height in order to guarantee the stability of the structure. Originally finished off with battlements, the upper terrace –which provides a spectacular view over the vast kingdom of Granada– was modified following the Christian conquest with the addition of a bell, which was used to alert citizens in case of danger and also helped regulate the work of the farmers.

THE NASRID PALACES

The Mexuar

A blend of cultures
Considered as one of the oldest areas of the Nasrid palaces, it is adorned with tiles added in the Christian era.

Originating from a Nasrid family settled in the City of Malaga, Ismail I became the Sultan of Granada in the year 1314 after overthrowing King Nasr, who in turn had come to the throne after having obliged his brother, Muhammad III, to abdicate. His manoeuvre to take control garnered numerous enemies, but finally the King gained the legitimacy he sought after managing to lead successful military campaigns such as the Battle of Elvira, which helped provide a respite from the advance of Christian armies. Thanks to this stability, the Nasrid leader could carry out a remodellation of areas such as religious education, the army, the administration of justice or public safety; and took on the task of solving the economic difficulties of the court by means of new taxes aimed at the Jews. The reformist ambition of Ismail I was also reflected in his decision to construct a palace, the Mexuar, on the north-western corner of the Alhambra, on some lands that were very close to the Alcazaba. The architectonic structure conserved is comprised of two large courtyards –which most likely led to rooms that were used for diverse purposes, such as royal offices– and the Mexuar Hall, which lends its name to the arrangement and refers to the council of Viziers that assisted the Sultan with legislative tasks. With the construction of the rest of the Nasrid Palaces, the Mexuar area probably lost its original residential use and took on activities of a more bureaucratic and judicial nature, but was maintained as a vital space for the daily functioning of the Alhambra, as evidenced by the numerous refurbishments undertaken by both future sultans and Christian monarchs.

The Mexuar Hall
Refurbished by kings Yusuf I and Muhammad V over the fourteenth century, the salon in which the Sultan and his advisors gathered and carried out justice in the Nasrid period evolved around four marble columns of narrow design that supported a lantern-cupola, responsible for an adequate supply of natural light into the space. From the late fifteenth century, with the arrival of the Catholic Monarchs, the Mexuar Hall lost its original layout and underwent great changes in order that it could carry out its new role as a chapel. This way, its decoration was altered, the cupola was dismantled in order to add an upper floor, windows were opened up and a lateral wall was knocked down in order that a balustrade could be installed for the choir.

<<
**Patio of the
Gilded Room**
Centred around a
marble fountain, it acts
as a transition space
between the Mexuar
Palace and the
Comares Palace.

The Mexuar's oratory

Originally separate from the Mexuar Hall, into which it was incorporated in the latter half of the nineteenth century, the oratory reserved for the use of the Sultan and those closest to him was designed to face Mecca, in order to fulfil the Muslim obligation to pray looking in the direction of Mohammed the Prophet's hometown. In its chevet is a *mihrab* –the niche in which the *Koran* is found– of polygonal ground plan preceding from a horseshoe-shaped arch on whose imposts is inscribed "Pray and do not be one of the disaffected", whilst along the length of the north wall –which is decorated with mottos in honour of Sultan Muhammad V– four windows were created with views of the Albaicín designed in order that worshippers could sit on the floor and rest their arms on the window ledge whilst contemplating the landscape.

The Gilded Room

Preceded by a triple archway portico leading to a courtyard adjoining the Mexuar, this space decorated during Muhammad V's reign was most likely used as a waiting room for visitors who waited to be received by the Sultan, though is it also believed to have been used by the secretaries of the court in charge of redacting the sentences dictated by the highest serving members of the Nasrid authority. The room's name is due to the coffering on the ceiling, which was repainted with golden ornamental details during the Christian period. The original design of the room was also altered with the creation of a lookout with seats facing eachother decorated with tilework.

THE NASRID PALACES

Comares Palace

Façade of Comares
Inaugurated in 1370, it was erected on the orders of Muhammad V to commemorate the conquest of Algeciras.

The kingdom of Granada experienced one of its most prosperous periods under the rule of Yusuf I, who came to the throne in order to substitute his brother Muhammad IV, assassinated in 1333. Described by Arab historians as a meditative leader of calm character, the seventh Sultan of the Nasrid dynasty was able to ward off attacks from Christian troops as well as the influence of the North-African emirs, guaranteeing a prolonged period of peace that was taken advantage of in order to provide the city with diverse public installations, such as primary schools, welfare centres and a *madrassah* or Islamic school that converted into one of the most important universities of the Islamic world. His fruitful reign welcomed the contributions of numerous intellectuals who were included in his court to help boost the development of the Sciences and Arts, consolidating Granada as a major centre of learning and knowledge. Within this context, it was inevitable that the Alhambra would undergo far-reaching changes aimed at reflecting the blossoming of Nasrid culture. Yusuf I prompted an ambitious construction scheme on the site that reached its peak with the creation of a new palace designed on the plots of land adjoining the Mexuar. Structured around a rectangular courtyard and presided over by a tower that contained the Throne Room, the largest room in the Alhambra, the space known as the Comares –which was completed by the son of the Sultan, Muhammad V– incorporated the elements most characteristic of Andalusian residences, at the same time as it converted into clear evidence of royal power by means of its symbolic ornamentation, considered one of the great milestones of Islamic architecture.

The staging of royal power

Apart from establishing a division between the palace's public space and private space, the Comares' façade was provided with a distinctive allegorical character thanks to its careful ornamentation, which was originally decorated with lively colours. Many of the epigraphic messages located on the façade illustrate passages from the Koran related to divine sovereignty, with a clear intention of consolidating the figure of the Sultan in a period of military triumphs, whilst the plant-life details help reinforce the image of the palace as a paradisiacal setting.

Tiling
Adorned with geometric designs, the baseboards of the porticos of the courtyard provide chromatic variety to the arrangement.

<<
North pavilion
The water's reflection underlines the importance of the entrance to the Throne Room.

The Court of the Myrtles

As was customary in Hispano-Muslim residential architecture, the internal communication of the Comares Palace was centred around a large rectangular courtyard that was probably finalised in the latter half of the 15th century, during the reign of Sultan Muhammad V. At the heart of this open space a large pond was planned flanked by parterres of myrtle bushes that contributed in a decisive way to lending a greater depth to the site, likewise highlighting the dimension of the surrounding buildings, which were clearly reflected in the water, the symbol of life and Muslim paradise. At the same time, the presence of the pond helped soften the atmosphere of the palace, acting as an element that provided a sensation of coolness and freshness and which facilitated the ventilation of the different areas around the patio.

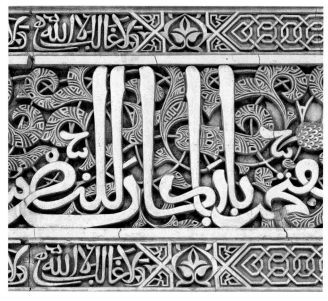

South pavilion

Possibly built to be used by the Sultan's heir, the rooms in this sector were partially destroyed in the fifteenth century in order to construct Charles V Palace, though the façade remains and acts as an architectonic backdrop. The first level of the façade is comprised of a gallery with seven archways decorated with epigraphs and plant-life details and geometric patterns, whilst the second floor has seven windows with wooden latticework that provide light to a long room. Lastly, the third floor consists of a gallery overlooking the Court of the Myrtles by means of seven arches and a larger central lintelled opening.

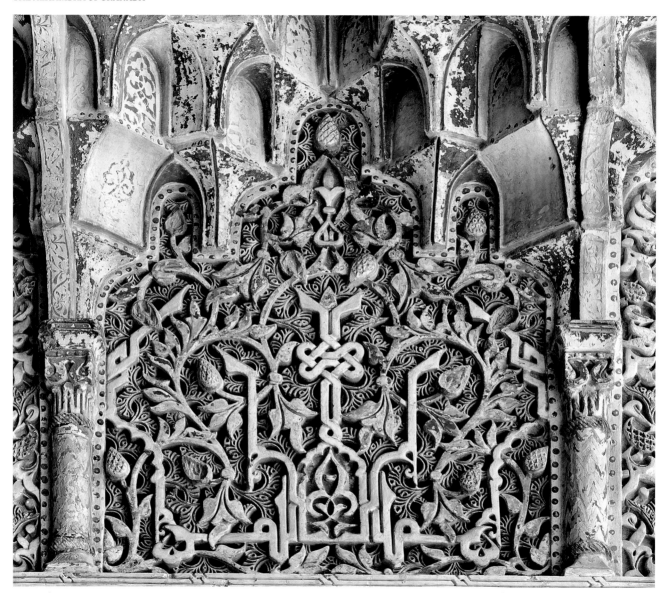

Decoration. Honeycomb work, plant details and religious poems adorn the entrance to the Hall of the Boat from the Court of the Myrtles.

Hall of the Boat. The skirting boards of the room that precedes the Throne Room are decorated with tiling, while the roof is provided with star-shaped forms.

Central room
This area was used by the Sultan, whose silhouette was outlined in the backlight of the window, which held a stained glass window.

Throne Room

Designed by Yusuf I in the Comares Tower's exterior, the most important room of the palace was the symbolic stage of the Sultan's power, who from his throne presided over the counsels of the realm and official receptions. With a square ground plan measuring 11.3 metres on each side, on three of the salon's walls are deeply set niches, designed for accommodating the supreme authorities. In the central room on the north side, opposite the main entrance, was the Sultan's throne, which boasted a privileged view of Granada and the Court of the Myrtles. In order to highlight the solemnity of the space, Nasrid craftsmen completely recovered the interior façades with tiled baseboards and plasterwork panels with plant-life patterns, geometric figures and inscriptions that were originally polychromed.

Interior. The compositions that decorate the walls and the ceiling of the Throne Room cause a kaleidoscope effect, emphasising the depth of the space.

Roofing

The decorative scheme of the Throne Room – and, by extension, of the Comares Palace– culminates with the room's squared ceiling, made up of seven symmetrical panels in which Nasrid cabinet-makers set 8,017 pieces of wood that make up a magnificent arrangement of stars. The composition can be interpreted as the representation of the Seven Heavens that, according to Islamic belief, must be crossed before arriving at the throne of God, represented by the cube of *muqarna* work that is found in the centre of the cupola. In this way, the ceiling directly related the Sultan with divine power, legitimising his authority whilst associating him with the idea of perfection.

Bathroom

In Islamic religion, body hygiene is fundamental, in such a way that Muslim cities and palaces were provided with baths, or *hamman*, spaces that apart from their spiritual connotations had a social purpose as well. In Comares, the baths –the only ones remaining in the Alhambra– were a space suitable for discussing affairs of the state in a relaxed atmosphere, far removed from the constrictions of more solemn rooms such as the Throne Room. With a structure inspired by Roman baths, the cleansing area was divided into four rooms: the first one was for undressing and resting, the second was used for carrying out ablutions (spiritual bathing), the third –the most spacious– was the steam room and the fourth, situated next to an oven, was provided with two basins with hot and cold water.

THE NASRID PALACES

The Palace of the Lions

Naturalism
Similar to a palm tree forest, the columns in the Court of the Lions convey the idea of earthly paradise.

The Nasrid kingdom continued its economic, political and cultural growth under the reign of Sultan Muhammad V, who took over the throne in 1354 after his father was assassinated whilst praying in the Alhambra's mosque. Despite being victim of family intrigues which even led to a brief exile five years after having been crowned, the Muslim monarch was able to keep up the peace policy initiated by his forefather and managed to provide stability to the Granadian territory thanks to his excellent relationship with King Peter I of Castile (Peter the Cruel or the Just) –with whom he established a serfdom pact– and his flair for diplomacy when faced with interference from North-African tribes in the affairs of the Nasrid court. Just like his predecessor, Muhammad V combined his governing facet with that of promoter of art and literature, surrounding himself with leading scholars such as the writer and historian Ibn al-Jatib and the poet Ibn Zamrak, whilst at the same time excelling as a constructor by directing the most spectacular transformation the Alhambra had ever undergone. With the willingness to demonstrate the greatness of his rule, the Sultan refurbished the area of the Mexuar and completed the decoration of Comares, though his main project was actually the building of the Palace of the Lions. Distinguished by the fountain that provides the site with its name, this work brought together all the achievements of Nasrid architecture by means of a masterful combination of ornamental elements that helped provide the different rooms in the complex with a refined and elegant appearance, in tune with the functions of relaxation and leisure traditionally attributed to them.

Temples
Pavilions with a square ground plan and wooden cupola were erected on the eastern and western sides of the courtyard.

Court of the Lions

As with the Comares site, the patio is the organising element of the Palace of the Lions, though in this case instead of a pond the centre is taken up with a fountain sculpture whose four spouts correspond with the cardinal points of the compass and which refer to the four rivers of Muslim paradise – the River Euphrates, the Nile, the Sihran and the Jihran–. With a layout that reminds of the design of benedictine monastery cloisters, the patio's perimeter is provided with an exquisitely decorated arcaded gallery that leads to different rooms. On the western side is the Hall of the Mocárabes; to the east, the Hall of the Kings; to the north, the Hall of the Two Sisters –which in turn leads to the Hall of the Ajimeces and the viewpoint Mirador de Lindaraja–, and to the south, the Hall of the Abencerrages.

Fountain of the Lions
Converted into the symbolic guardians of the Sultan's power, a dozen lions carved from white marble contemplate and guard each and every corner of the courtyard whilst their jaws spurt out streams of water, which represents life and the beginning and end of everything. On the animals' backs is a dodecagonal shaped (twelve-sided) basin, on whose edges are engraved verses by Ibn Zamrak, the poet of the court of Muhammad V. By means of beautiful metaphors, the texts praise and honour the figure of the Sultan and allude to the ingenious hydraulic system of the fountain, which meant that the basin's water level was always the same. The fountain underwent numerous modifications from the sixteenth century, when new elements were introduced in order to adapt it to changing tastes. Finally, in the year 1966 it was given back its original structure.

Gallery

The archways that make up the corridor bordering the Court of the Lions are supported by 124 Macael marble columns that appear individually as well as in pairs or groups of three or four, generating a harmonious composition that provides the arrangement with a dynamic feel. The expressivity of the space is highlighted by detailed ornamentation of all the architectonic elements, which despite their apparent uniformity are quite distinct in their decorative style, carried out based on caligraphies, plant-life details and geometric patterns.

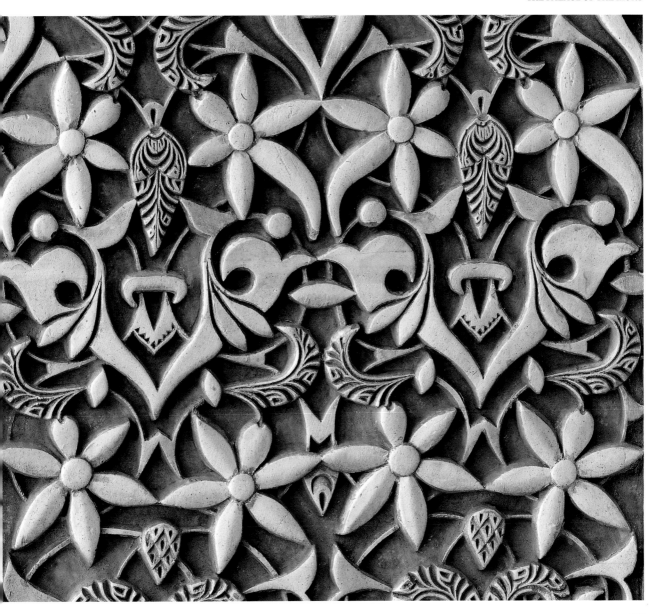

The Hall of the Abencerrages

The area that closes off the south side of the Court of the Lions owes its name to the ancient belief that it was there that nobles from the Abencerrages clan were assassinated in the fifteenth century. It is comprised of a central square-shaped room and two side bed-chambers used as a rest area. In the centre of the room is a dodecag-onal marble fountain that receives light coming from the patio as well as the lattice work that is situated in the upper part of the roof, which is a cupola with mocárabes of eight pointed star-shaped forms that can be inter-preted as an allegory of the universe.

vocative ambience
he alternation of the
rches that divide the
terior of the room
ean that there is an
teresting play of light
nd shadow.

<
ault
ecorated with
ocárabes, it covers
ne of the main rooms
f the Hall of the Kings.

Hall of the Kings

On the side of the Court of the Lions a rectangularly shaped room measuring over thirty metres long was constructed that, owing to its dimensions, is believed to have been used in order to celebrate parties and banquets. The space is divided up by *mocárabe* archways in seven distinct stretches. Finished off with separate vaults that protrude from the roof in a lantern style and connected to the patio by means of porticos, the three larger sized areas have three rectangular bedchambers covered with elliptic domed ceilings decorated with paintings. In one of them a meeting between eminent Muslims is depicted, whilst in the other two works are scenes of knighthood and court life theme. The author of these works is unknown, though various writers have suggested the influence of the great Italian masters.

Vaults. Constructed with wood, the three vaults of the eastern chamber are decorated with paintings that represent scenes from court life.

Tempera painting. From high up in the tower a lady, with pleading gesture, contemplates a duel between her two suitors, a Christian and a Muslim.

The Hall of the Two Sisters

Two monumental arches lead into what is considered the main room of the palace, baptised as the Hall of the Two Sisters for the marble flagstones within the floor that flank the low central fountain. This space is also believed to have been the place where the royal council was held, though it also might have had an eminently residential use, in line with the private character that has traditionally been attributed to the Palace of the Lions. Provided with lateral chambers that had beds and a higher floor adorned with latticework, the room stands out for its octagonal-shaped cupola, made up of a total of 5,416 mocárabe pieces –originally polychromed– that receive the sunlight coming from the openings in the tambour.

Symbolic decoration
On the walls of the Hall of the Two Sisters, over the tiled baseboard that decorates the lower stretch with geometric figures, one of the longest inscriptions found on the Alhambra site can be seen, comprised of twenty-four verses laid out in rectangular and medallion shaped consoles. Originating from a poem composed by the great Visir Ibn Zamrak on the occasion of the circumcision of the son of Sultan Muhammad V, the texts refer to the beauty of the palace, defined as a "beautiful building" which "exceeds, peradventure, all those that have been built before".

Mirador de Lindaraja

A small room of square ground plan designed on the north side of the Hall of the Two Sisters functioned as a gallery with views over the exterior gardens and Granada. According to tradition, this room was the place of relaxation for the Sultan's favourite wife, given that its name originates from the Arabic words *Ayn Dar Aixa*, which can be translated as "Eyes of the House of Aixa". Decorated with numerous epigraphical inscriptions, both the central window –with double arch and mullion– and the side ones are installed quite low down, in order that the people occupying the room can admire the landscape whilst they are sitting on the floor. The type of ceiling used was a wooden framework with incrusted coloured glass work that reflects the light of the upper windows, reinforcing the palatial character of this look-out point.

Vault
The pieces of glass are assembled in a pine wooden frame structure with the shape of an upside down trough.

Hall of the Ajimeces

The area of transition between the Hall of the Two Sisters and the Mirador de Lindaraja is this space of rectangular ground plan whose name derives from the two windows in the north wall, which possibly originally had wooden balconies with lattice work. The lower stretch of the walls, now bare, were covered with silk tapestries during the Muslim period, while the upper part still maintains the plasterwork with religious inscriptions and the coats of arms from the Nasrid kingdom. The vault ceiling adorned with mocárabes was reconstructed during the sixteenth century.

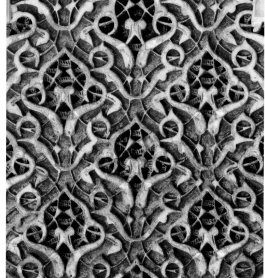

Christian chambers

Cherub
Inspired by the Italian Renaissance, it is part of the pictorial decoration of the Queen's Dressing Room.

Following a decade of war, in 1492 the Catholic Monarchs conquered the city of Granada, culminating their project which was to take over all the territories on the Iberian peninsula that had been under Muslim control. As a sign of their appreciation of the Nasrid architectonic legacy and eager to provide lasting evidence of their military victory, the Castilian-Aragonese monarchs financed a series of architectonic refurbishments that were designed to guarantee the conservation of the Alhambra, which had been subject to quite a lot of damage during the hard siege it underwent. The majority of interventions consisted of the renovation of damaged ceilings, the replacement of paving and the reinforcement of walls, although new rooms and decorative elements were also built, such as the stairs and passages that helped connect spaces that up until that time had been isolated. The grandson of the Catholic Monarchs, Emperor Charles V, remained faithful to the idea of safeguarding the palatine city as a symbol of royal power, even though he was more ambitious than his predecessors by planning the construction of a new palace to become the headquarters for his court. In order to accommodate the monarch whilst work on his future residence was being carried out, between the years 1528 and 1537 diverse rooms were built around the Comares Palace and the Palace of the Lions, connected by means of a corridor and facing an irregularly shaped courtyard. Perfectly blending in with the rest of the rooms of Nasrid origin, the new chambers converted into a reflection of the dynamism of the Alhambra, a site accustomed to adapting to the passing of history.

The Emperor's rooms

After deciding that the Alhambra would accommodate his new palace, in the year 1528 Charles V approved the construction of six new chambers distributed around the Court of the Lindaraja. In contrast to the sumptuous appearance of the Nasrid palaces, the new rooms were characterised by their austere and more simple design, perfectly suited to the Emperor's lifestyle. Identified as an office and equipped with a large hearth, the first room of the complex was joined to an antechamber through which the royal bedrooms could be accessed, which in turn led to the adjoining two Halls of Fruit, so-called for the paintings that decorate the hexagonal panels of the wooden ceilings.

Classicism
Illuminated by nine windows, the Queen's Dressing Room is very similar in appearance to Italian rooms of the same with fresco work decorating its walls.

The Queen's Dressing Room

In the framework of the refurbishments programmed in order to accommodate Emperor Charles V in the Alhambra, in the upper part of the ancient tower of Abu-I-Hayyay –which might have been used as a zone for recreation and meditation during the Nasrid period– a private chamber was created in the year 1537 for Empress Isabella, who in the end never actually used the room. Surrounded by a

Renaissance style gallery that provides a panoramic view of the Darro River valley and which is decorated with mural paintings of lively, vibrant colour, this space was to be called the "heater of the Royal Houses", given that on one of its far ends there was a perforated slab whose holes filtered the smoke and perfume that came from the aromatic essences burnt in the chimney that was located in the room down below.

Paintings

Trained in the *atelier* of Renaissance master Raphael, painters of Italian origin Julio Aquiles and Alejandro Mayner were commissioned with decorating the Queen's Dressing Room between the years 1539 and 1544. They drew their inspiration from mythological scenes taken from Ovid's *Metamorphoses*, cherubs, plant-life and allegorical animals, such as griffons or two-headed eagles. Likewise, with the aim to highlight the figure of Charles V, the artists carried a sequence of eight pictures based on the sketches of Jan Cornelisz Vermeyen that recreate the Conquest of Tunis by Imperial troops, from the departure from the Port of Cagliari to the triumphant return to the Italian city of Trapani.

Court of the Grated Window. Presided by a marble fountain, it is believed to have been planned between 1654 and 1655 to facilitate access to adjoining areas.

The Partal

In 1302 the Nasrid throne was taken over by Muhammad III, who brought stability to the kingdom of Granada on the Iberian peninsula by means of a truce agreed with King Ferdinand IV of Castile. Moreover, he successfully led various incursions into North African territory. Despite his concern for keeping Moorish dominions united, the Sultan had to abdicate seven years after coming to power, debilitated by lack of insight and the victim of an internal conspiration hatched by his brother Nasr. Nonetheless, the brevity of his reign did not hinder his numerous urban development plans for the Alhambra, where, as well as erecting a mosque, he is thought to have been behind the construction of the palatial site of the Partal – whose name derives from the Arabic term *al-Bartal*, which means "portico"–. Located around a section of the northern wall, the royal chambers were probably subject to refurbishments and extensions, and surrounding these were other buildings aimed at Nasrid leaders, such as the Palace of Yusuf III, which after the Christian conquest converted into the residence of the governors or *alcaides* of the fortress. With the passing of time, most of the constructions of the Muslim period were destroyed –except the palace that lends its name to the area, an oratory and some small two-storey Moorish houses–, in such a way that the original layout of the site was lost. From the twentieth century, the public-sector managers of the Alhambra carried out the acquisition and expropriation of the lands of the Partal that were private property, with the objective of rehabilitating the entire area and integrating the archeological remains into a landscaped garden of great aesthetic value.

A natural setting
Of modern creation, the gardens going around the Palace of the Partal hide the site's urban origins.

Palace of the Portico
With a layout that adheres to the Comares Palace, the Partal complex –which would have originally encompassed more buildings– is presided over by a rectangular courtyard whose pond's north side borders the arcaded portico that the palace is named after. Structured around five canted archways –the central one is of a larger size–, the porch leads to a square-shaped room decorated with tiled skirting boards and plasterwork that include some of the most ancient inscriptions of the Alhambra. The salon has a 16-sided central cupola, very similar to what was designed on the observation point of the tower that tops the site.

Decoration. The arrangement includes plasterwork with allegorical inscriptions on the arches and walls, as well as tiled skirting boards and ceilings with geometric designs.

Oratory

On the wall coming from the Palace of the Partal, a free-standing tower of rectangular ground plan, with the function of private oratory, was built between 1333 and 1354, coinciding with the reign of Sultan Yusuf I. A midsection generated by a semicircular arch leads to the small prayer area, on whose south-east wall – facing Mecca– is a mihrab or niche with a canted horseshoe arch covered by a dome of mocárabes and intricately decorated in plaster with exquisite epigraphs that refer to different passages from the Koran. The room, with a roof that faces all points of the compass and built with brick, blended in perfectly with the natural landscape with the aim of aiding the Sultan's meditation. From inside, where the coffered ceiling stands out, the landscape can be viewed through two lateral windows.

Art in plaster
The interior of the oratory stands out for the fine plasterwork that decorates the mihrab and the walls of the room.

Gardens

During the first third of the 20th century land-scaped gardens were created in the area of the Partal that in the Muslim period had included residences of some of the most influential Nasrid families. Therefore, archeological remains preserved as evidence of Nasrid splendour were high-lighted and embel-lished by an abundance of rich vegetation, fountains, ponds and canals perfectly adapt-ed to the staggered, stepped structure of the land. At the same time, new gardens helped link up the internal traffic of the Alhambra in a much more efficient way, channelling movement between the sector of the Nasrid palaces and the upper zone of the Medina.

The Medina

Nasrid leaders were able to carry out their daily activities thanks to the support of a healthy number of civil servants, house staff and craftsmen who focused all their efforts on the needs of the court. These subjects of the realm were responsible for a multitude of tasks such as the maintenance of palace properties, administrative duties related to the governing of the realm, the supply of raw materials and the manufacture of textile and decorative products, amongst other responsibilities, which meant that it was much more practical to accommodate them on the Alhambra site. Therefore, between the thirteenth and fifteenth centuries, an urban development similar to any Muslim city began to take shape within the walled perimeter. Provided with a mosque in which inhabitants carried out prayer rituals and received important news, the neighbourhood's structure was based around a street going from West to East, whose origin was in a residential area probably aimed at high-ranking employees and which ended up in a more working-class zone, comprised of properties and workshops specialised in ceramic work, glass work and the leather and tanning industry. From 1492, with the Christian arrival, all these constructions underwent complete refurbishment –or were even demolished– in order to make way for new buildings such as the Church of Saint Mary, which meant the citadel lost its original layout. Traces of its Muslim past were even more hidden away in 1812, when Napoleonic troops destroyed a large area of the higher area of the Alhambra, transforming it into a wasteland that could not be redeveloped until the 20th century when an ambitious archeological project got underway.

A double window
Situated on the interior façade of the Wine Gate, it displays the Nasrid coat of arms with the motto "Only God is the Victor".

The Wine Gate

Most likely constructed in the fourteenth century, during the reign of King Muhammad III, the main entrance of the Medina coincided with the start of the street that directed the internal traffic of the urban centre of the citadel. Owing to its location, within the walled perimeter, the gateway did not need to take on the curved design that was characteristic of the exterior entranceways of the Alhambra and it was therefore planned with a straight outline. Moreover, inside the actual gateway were benches for the soldiers on guard –who were also provided with another space above on the upper floor–, whilst on the façades there were inscriptions and allegorical reliefs, such as the key that decorates the lintel of the western façade.

Qubba
Decorated with inscriptions, the central salon of the ancient Nasrid palazzo had an observation point with views over the Generalife.

Saint Francis Convent

During the Muslim period, the east zone of the upper Medina was presided over by a small palace of a distinguished member of the Nasrid nobility. Probably built during the reign of Sultan Muhammad II and refurbished in the period of Muhammad V, the building was made up of four enfilades going around a rectangular courtyard with a pond, and also had vegetable gardens and bathrooms. In the year 1495, following the arrival of the Christians, the site converted into a Franciscan convent and a main chapel was constructed in the former main room of the Nasrid property, in which the Catholic Monarchs were laid to rest until 1521, when they were later transferred to the Royal Chapel of Granada. Some centuries later, it was used as a prison and residence for the poor, until it was finally reopened in 1945 in the form of a hotel.

<
Saint Mary's of the Alhambra
Built between 1581 and 1618 by architect Ambrosio Vico and based on a design by Juan de Herrera, *Santa Maria de la Alhambra* took over the area of the largest mosque of the Alhambra, which had been erected in the 14th century on the orders of Sultan Muhammad III and which was demolished by Christian authorities in 1576. With a simple façade made from brick and concrete, the temple was based around a Latin cross, with just one nave flanked by six chapels. In 1671, a baroque style altarpiece was put in the apse that since the mid 18th century has been home to a statue of the Virgin of Anguish, also called "Our Lady of Sorrows".

>
Mosque's bath
Situated on Calle Real, it was constructed in the times of Muhammad III next to the main mosque. Today part of the structure is conserved that had various rooms and side chambers.

Charles V Palace

Initiator of the Hapsburg dynasty in Spain and author of the most important empire of his time, Charles V first came into contact with Granada in 1526, when he spent his honeymoon there after celebrating his marriage in Seville with Isabella of Portugal. Despite having grown up in the Netherlands, the Catholic Monarchs' grandson quickly grew to appreciate how symbolically important the former capital of the Nasrid realm was for the Spanish Crown and, amazed by the beauty of the Alhambra, decided to erect his own residence in the palatine city, which was to convert into a symbol of religious unity at a time marked by conflicts with the Ottomans and by divisions caused by the Protestant Reformation. The design of the palace –identified with the name *Casa Real Nueva* (New Royal House), in contrast to the *Casa Real Vieja* (Old Royal House), referring to the buildings of Muslim origin– was carried out by Pedro Machuca. Trained in Italy with artists such as Michelangelo, the architect devised a Renaissance monumental style edifice, incorporating a circular courtyard within a square ground plan. Defrayed with the contributions of Moriscos (Moors converted to Christianity after the Spanish Reconquest), the work started in 1527, but could not be completed on time. Machuca died when he had only erected a part of the exterior, whilst Charles V hardly had time to concern himself with the progress of the work due to constant political and economic conflicts he had to tackle. The successors of the Emperor let the project languish due to funding problems, and it wasn't until the twentieth century that pending building work could be finished on the palace, which adopted a new use as a museum.

Contrast
The palace's Renaissance style forms provide a contrast to the constructions of Muslim origin.

Western façade. Presided by the coat of arms of Philip II, the main entrance of the palace combines pillars of Doric order with Ionic columns.

outh façade

ymbols of royal power,
e lions appear on
culptures that flank
e entrance doorway
nd they are also depic-
ed on wall rings.

Exterior of the palace

In accordance with the ideals of classical proportions, the façades that make up the exterior of the Charles V Palace are divided at horizontal level into two sections, differentiated by their architectonic and decorative treatment. On the lower level, architect Pedro Machuca integrated pillars into a wall with cushioned ashlars to convey an image of solidness whilst the upper floor, related to the royal chambers, took on a more refined appearance by means of the use of Ionic columns and the lintelled openings with pediments, which were combined with emblems and allegorical reliefs. At the same time, in order to highlight the entranceways located on the southern and western façades –which were in turn the most exposed– arcaded passages in the style of victory arches were created.

Allegorical decoration

The iconographic programme of the façades of the palace was devised in order to highlight the virtues of Charles V by means of diverse reliefs inspired by historical and mythological themes. Thus on the western façade of the palace –the most monumental– war episodes are depicted protagonised by the Emperor, as well as various scenes from the works of *Hercules* and representations of *Fame, Abundance and Victory*. Likewise, the southern façade –which leads to the Emperor's chambers– includes the figures of the Gods Neptune and Amphitrite, in a possible allegory to the maritime power of the monarch.

Courtyard

The interior of the palace is made up of a large circular-shaped courtyard of Roman style delimited by an adjacent corridor which, just like on the exterior, is organised into two floors, each one of them connected with the different rooms and comprised of thirty-two stone columns. On the lower level, the pillars are of Doric-Tuscan style and support an entablature with metopes and triglyphs, whilst the colonnade on the upper floor adopts the Ionic style order and is bordered by a closed balustrade.

Upper gallery. Its construction was completed in 1967, when the flat wooden ceiling was installed over the passage overlooking the courtyard.

The Generalife

Leisure space
Water and plant-life provided the perfect atmosphere for the Sultan to forget about his preoccupations.

Since they settled in the Iberian peninsula, the Muslim elites were characterised for possessing large properties named *almúnyas* (vegetable gardens or farms), usually situated in the periphery of the cities and comprised of a residential centre surrounded by vast expanses of land used as pastures for grazing and for the cultivation of horticultural products and fruit trees. One of the functions of these complexes was to highlight the privileged status of their owners, who also turned to their properties to escape from the hectic lifestyle of the court by means of activities such as hunting, walking or contemplation. On the other hand, the *almúnyas* also provided economic benefits by means of agricultural and livestock farming, laying the foundations of a model that is still present in numerous parts of Andalusia. In the case of the kingdom of Granada, one of the most important *almúnyas* was that of the Generalife, whose name possibly originates from the Arabic expression *Yannat-al-Arif*, which can be translated as "the garden of the architect". Situated on a hill near to the northern walls of the Alhambra, from which it was separated by a ravine, the estate of the Nasrid kings embraced at least four large vegetable gardens –irrigated by the same canal that supplied the palatine city– and had lands suitable for farm animals and horsebreeding. The areas reserved for the Sultan –which were probably erected in the late thirteenth century, on the initiative of Muhammad II– were integrated in a harmonious way into the wild environment, forming an arrangement of great beauty that evolved in tandem with the Alhambra by means of the changes introduced by successive inhabitants.

The palace

Originally planned with a cross-shape layout, a courtyard of rectangular ground plan crossed longitudinally by the *Acequia Real* (Royal Irrigation Ditch) constitutes the central nucleus of the Palace of the Generalife. In the Muslim period, the western side was completely closed off by a high wall, substituted in the Christian era by an open gallery; whilst the eastern side was delimited by a passage that led to the bathrooms. Totally remodelled, the pavilion that borders with the south side of the patio could possibly have been used for the rooms of the concubines. The north pavilion, in contrast, constitutes the principal aristocratic space of the site, by including the rooms used by the Sultan.

Interior of the pavilion
The decoration of the portico and Royal Chamber (*Salón Regio*) alludes to the occupants' status.

North pavilion

The Sultan's chambers were found at the head of the Patio of the Irrigation Ditch (Patio de la Acequia), in a pavilion made up of a portico with five archways that leads to the Royal Chamber. Provided with lateral bedchambers, this area might have been used by the Nasrid King to attend urgent affairs, likewise for receiving guests that visited the property to relax and unwind. The main axis of the hall was modified in 1319 with the addition of a tower designed by Sultan Ismail I after his victory in the Battle of Sierra Elvira and which is decorated with epigraphs that refer to the glory of God. The transformation of the pavilion was even more extensive towards the end of the fifteenth century, when the Catholic Monarchs carried out an extension that supposed the construction of an upper floor and a Renaissance style open gallery.

>
**The Court of
the Sultana's
Cypress Tree**
The north pavilion of
the Palace of the Gener-
alife connects with a
courtyard in which a
small square pond
stands out with a foun-
tain that in turn is sur-
rounded by a u-shaped
pool of water full of
water jets. This space
–which, according to
tradition, was the scene
of meetings between
sultán Muley Hacén's
wife and her lover– has
undergone more modi-
fications since the Nas-
rid period, when it is
believed to have held
the baths of the palace,
completely destroyed by
the Christian occupants.

<
South pavilion
Above a structured
portico based on five
brick archways is a sec-
ond level that holds a
rectangular room
boasting an observation
point overlooking
the Patio of the
Irrigation Ditch.

ower gardens. Built between 1931 and 1951 in a former vegetable garden, it emulates Muslim gardens, with ornamental fountains and ponds.

THE ALHAMBRA OF GRANADA
THE ART OF ARCHITECTURE

CONCEPT AND MANAGEMENT OF PROJECT: CARLOS GIORDANO AND NICOLÁS PALMISANO
CONTENTS: DANIEL R. CARUNCHO
PHOTOGRAPHIC RETOUCHING: JAVIER ORDUÑA / AIDA JIMENEZ DE LA ROCHA

PUBLISHED BY
© DOS DE ARTE EDICIONES, S.L., BARCELONA, 2017

TEXTS
MANAGEMENT AND COORDINATION: DOS DE ARTE EDICIONES, S.L.
WRITER: DANIEL R. CARUNCHO
TRANSLATION: CERYS GIORDANO JONES
© DOS DE ARTE EDICIONES, S.L., BARCELONA, 2017

PHOTOGRAPHS
AUTHORS: CARLOS GIORDANO AND NICOLÁS PALMISANO
© DOS DE ARTE EDICIONES, S.L., BARCELONA, 2017

ARCHIVE IMAGES
• PAGE 7. © PACO AYALA / PHOTAKI.COM
• PAGE 8. FRAGMENT OF AN ENGRAVING BY HOEFNAGEL FROM 1575. ALBUM/AKG/HISTORIC-MAPS
• PAGE 9. ENGRAVING BY DAVID ROBERTS DATING AROUND 1835. ALBUM/SFGP
• PAGE 63. ALBUM/UNIVERSAL IMAGES GROUP/WERNER FORMAN
• PAGES 82-83. ALBUM/ORONOZ

ACKNOWLEDGEMENTS
DOS DE ARTE EDICIONES THANKS PATRONATO DE LA ALHAMBRA Y GENERALIFE
FOR ITS COLLABORATION IN THE REALISATION OF THIS BOOK.

EDITION 2017

ISBN: 978-84-9103-016-4
LEGAL DEPOSIT: B 2943-2017
PRINTED IN SPAIN

PEFC Certified

This product is
from sustainably
managed forests and
controlled sources

PEFC/14-38-00202   www.pefc.es